Even If...

TRUSTING IN GOD EVEN IF
THE UNTHINKABLE HAPPENS

DEBORAH T. RIPLEY

iUniverse

EVEN IF...
TRUSTINGINGODEVENIFTHEUNTHINKABLEHAPPENS

iUniverse books may be ordered through booksellers or by contacting:

iUniverse
1663 Liberty Drive
Bloomington, IN 47403
www.iuniverse.com
1-800-Authors (1-800-288-4677)

ISBN: 978-1-4917-7509-7 (sc)
ISBN: 978-1-4917-7510-3 (e)

Library of Congress Control Number: 2015916673

Print information available on the last page.

iUniverse rev. date: 10/19/2015

Lovingly dedicated to my sweetheart,
husband and best friend,

Ed

Contents

FROM MY HEART . . .

I could not have made it through this time of my life without the love and support of so many people.

First, my children: Rachael, Alan, Amber and Ryan. They have walked through this with me and continue to love and support me in all I do. I could never have gotten through this without you. I am blessed beyond measure to have you as my children. There are not enough words to express my love for you. Always remember, I love you more. . . . .

One of the greatest blessings in my life is to be *MiMi* to three wonderful grandchildren: Charlotte, Lylah and Seth. They have brought such joy to my life and another level of love I didn't understand until I became a grandmother. I will be blessed to be MiMi again this fall to Arabella Grace! I love all of you more...

I am blessed to have been brought up in a Christian home by wonderful, loving parents, Allen and Nellie Treadway, who taught me about Jesus and how to trust Him. I am still blessed to have them in my life. They have always supported me and still do with unconditional love. I love you both so very much.

I am so thankful for my brother, Greg, sister-in-love, Diane, and my beautiful nieces, Cortnie and Jennifer. They came by the hospital many nights and brought food and took care of our needs. They continue to support me.

I know I can always depend on them. I love you all so very much.

Pastor Chris and Sis. Renita Warren and the Amazing Grace Ministries choir and congregation have loved and supported me through the many rough seasons that go along with losing someone. I will always be thankful that God directed me to you. You are family and always will be. I love you.

Pastors Myles and DeLana Rutherford and my Worship With Wonders family were a spiritual haven for me during this time. Thank you for your love and support. I am blessed to call 3WC home and am excited to begin the next season of my life with you!

To all the family who financially made this book possible, I thank you from the bottom of my heart! I pray you are blessed beyond measure.

And to all who have lost someone they love – I pray somehow my story touches you and brings healing to your heart…*EVEN IF.*

INTRODUCTION

The Journey Begins

I have always loved to read. As a young child I remember the excitement I would feel when I could order books from the book club at school. One year for my birthday my parents subscribed to a yearly book club where I received a new book every month. I still have many of those books today. I love to read.

Writing, on the other hand, has never been something that interested me. I always did well on my writing assignments in school but that was something I had to do. I didn't do it because I enjoyed it.

I have never been one to keep a journal, but during this time in my life, God told me to do so. Sometimes important things happen that we forget as time passes. So from the time of my husband, Ed's, diagnosis I wrote. Not every day, but often.

It is my prayer that somehow my story will bring you hope and healing...*EVEN IF.*

JOURNAL ENTRY - MARCH 9, 2010

"In the midst of this trial, I am impressed by God to keep a journal. So many things happen that you remember at the

time, but may be forgotten as time goes by. These times are important..."

Have you documented your journey? It may help someone...*EVEN IF.*

CHAPTER ONE

Our Love Story

Ed and I met at church and started going together when I was 14 and he was 17. That consisted of sitting together in church and maybe talking on the phone once a week! You've got to remember this was before cell phones and you were charged for long-distance calls. We lived about an hour's drive from each other.

As we got older, we dated by going to fellowship meetings and youth events together. He was the only boy I ever dated. We became engaged when I was 16 but waited until I graduated from high school at 17 to be married. He was 20.

We literally grew up together. We were young, but we had a strong love and a determination that withstood many trials and situations that are a normal part of marriage.

We were blessed with three amazing children, Rachael, Alan and Ryan, and we were living the American dream. We both had businesses that we had created and we worked very hard. It was normal to go home tired at the end of the day. We worked together so we were with each other 24/7. Not all married couples could do this but we had done it for several years and we loved it. We built a home on some acreage and enjoyed raising cattle, gardening and taking care of our horses. Life was good.

Early in our marriage Ed felt the call of God on his life to minister. Through the years we had the privilege of serving in various churches as youth and children's ministry pastors. We made so many precious friends through the years. In 1995 we helped to begin a summer camp for children and youth from the churches we had ministered in.

Our children were always a vital part of our ministry. They helped in so many ways: music, art, drama, dance and production. We could not have accomplished all we did for the kingdom of God without them.

We were blessed to be able to home school them so we were together more than what most families are. We were and still are a very close family. I am so thankful for all of the time we were able to spend together. Little did we know that Ed's time would be cut short.

CHAPTER TWO

It Will Be Well

In 2005, I wrote these words which were inspired by God. I didn't realize at the time that they would be words *I* would be encouraged by.

"It Will Be Well"

Four little words that contain such power and hope,
It will be well.
A promise seems to be slipping away.
Something longed for for so long,
Now only a memory.
A what might have been?
But she chose to see not what was, but what would be.
It will be well.
We know the power of life and death is in the tongue.
What will you choose to confess today?
Life or death?
It will be well or It's too late.
It will be well or The doctor says.
It will be well or What will we do now?
Walk through your test with these
four words as your daily prayer
It will be well.
And when that prayer is answered,

> Praise God with these three little words,
> *It is well*!
> II Kings 4:8-36 (King James Version)

This Bible passage speaks of the Shunammite woman. She was a well-to-do woman who built a room for the Prophet Elisha to use when he came to Shunem to minister. She would feed Elisha and his servant, Gehazi, and Elisha would rest in his room on the roof. The Bible doesn't say specifically how long this arrangement went on but one day Elisha asked his servant, "*What can we do for this woman to repay her kindness?*" Now this woman was a woman of means and she had no need for anything. She had a home and everything else she needed – except for a child.

When Gehazi told Elisha this, Elisha told the woman, "*About this time next year, you will hold a son in your arms.*" The woman said, "*Don't mislead your servant O man of God*" or in other words *please don't promise me something you can't control*. But just as Elisha had said, the next year she was holding her son in her arms.

Several years went by with the child growing as a child should. One day he wanted to go to his father who was out in the field with the reapers. While there, he complained of a headache and his father had a servant carry him home to his mother. The boy sat in his mother's lap until noon and then he died.

His mother took him up to the room of the Prophet Elisha and laid him on the bed. Then she called her husband and asked for one of the servants and a donkey so she could go to the man of God. When asked how everything was she responded, "*It will be well.*"

Her son, the child given by God, lies in a little upstairs room dead. She knew what happened. She knew what it *looked like* with the natural eye. But she also remembered where this child came from and responded, *It will be well.*

As she is approaching Elisha, he sees her and sends Gehazi to see what is wrong. She replies, "*It is well*" and continues to go to the man of God. When she reached Elisha she said, "*Did I ask you for a son? Didn't I tell you not to get my hopes up?*"

Elisha immediately knew what was wrong and instructed his servant to take his cloak and place it over the boy. But that was not enough for the Shunammite mother. She demanded the man of God to go to her son.

When he got to the home of the Shunammite woman, he laid himself across the body of the child and the boy's body became warm. The boy sneezed seven times and opened his eyes. He was restored to the mother who saw things not as they seemed, but as they would be.

JOURNAL ENTRY - FEBRUARY 26, 2010

"After several weeks of fighting a body rash and being in pain, Ed agrees to go to the emergency room. He was having severe pain in his right side and we thought it was his appendix. After a CT scan, it is diagnosed as a mass on his right kidney that needs further tests. It could be a pool of blood where he lifted something too heavy. It was the size of a baseball. The doctor said it 'looked suspicious.' They admit him to the hospital for further tests. He's in tremendous pain even though he's on morphine. He is scheduled for another CT scan. They send him home with pain medication."

CHAPTER THREE
The Nightmare Begins

"Thus begins a week of waiting for another CT scan with the hope that everything is going to be okay. I try to keep him as comfortable as possible and keep him medicated until we go for the other scan. Even though the doctor marked his file as 'urgent,' it is five days until the scan is done. Ed made it through great, he's such a trooper. The doctor said to come to his office on Tuesday for the scan results. Ed didn't want to tell anyone what the doctor suspected. He wanted to wait until we knew the test results. People began to pray."

I am a firm believer that the power of life and death is in the tongue, so I never spoke anything but total healing for

Ed, *It will be well*! Each day was a challenge as we waited to get the report from the doctor. We were in a state of shock, of denial. This couldn't be happening to us – to Ed. This happened to other people, to other families, not ours.

We both believed he would receive a good report from the doctor. There was just no way what the doctor suspected, could be true!

JOURNAL ENTRY - MARCH 9, 2010

"We make it through the weekend and find ourselves in the doctor's office. When the doctor comes in, I know what he's going to say. The preliminary pathology results are lymphoma – CANCER. We will need to meet with an oncologist to discuss treatment. And that was that. No small talk, no how are? Just – you have cancer.

But the truth of the matter was, I knew before the doctor ever said the words because God had quickened those words in my spirit just two nights earlier. I was walking through my living room around midnight and a medical show was on television. As I walked by the TV the person said, 'he has survived lymphoma,' and my heart just jumped. Lymphoma – not a word I had ever really thought about. But when the doctor told us 'you have lymphoma' I said 'Thank you God for the warning'."

CHAPTER FOUR

Living with the Diagnosis

JOURNAL ENTRY - MARCH 10, 2010

"When you hear the word cancer, your heart just kind of stops. You relate the term cancer with death. And even though you know in your heart that you serve a healing God, it still, for a moment, scares you and you ask 'why' but then you remember 'It will be well'. The Shunammite woman knew her child was lying on a bed upstairs dead, she had placed him there. He had died in her arms. But when asked how things were she responded, 'It will be well'. It looked bleak right then, it was scary, but she knew the power of the man of God."

When telling friends and family about the diagnosis, I would always end with *Ed's going to be healed* or *he's going to be fine* and I totally believed it. Even in our darkest time, I never gave up – we would just pray harder!

We both believed in the power of prayer and in the healing power of Jesus Christ. So when God spoke to me the day of Ed's diagnosis and said *you will get through this* I thought He meant that Ed would be healed. I couldn't imagine *getting through it* any other way!

JOURNAL ENTRY - MARCH 12, 2010

"It's Friday, March 12th, two weeks from the weekend in the ER, one week from the diagnosis. I checked with the doctor's office today to see if they have heard from the oncologist. They still don't have the pathologist's report. Perhaps God is working already! Perhaps the pre-diagnosis is wrong? Whatever comes our way - God is faithful."

Ed had always been a strong man of faith. When someone needed him to pray the 'prayer of faith' for them, he was always there. He believed with his whole heart in the power of prayer and in the healing power of the Great Physician. I could walk into our bedroom any time of the day or night and I'd hear him calling on the name of Jesus. That name brought him such comfort and assurance. Even in his pain, he knew that he wasn't alone. Jesus Christ was with him. And I felt the same assurance.

It wasn't just words. I declared that he was going to be fine. He was healed in Jesus name.

When you get a diagnosis like that, does it scare you? Sure it does. Do you get emotional? Sure you do. But you have to remember that even though the circumstances look one way to the human eye, God sees it through His eyes. There is nothing too hard for my God!

Ed loved to tease and joke around. I used to say I knew he was mad at me if he wasn't teasing me. It was one of his ways of showing his love.

When I look back at those days before his diagnosis, I remember him saying *"You're gonna miss me when I'm gone"*. I'd smile and say *"You're not going anywhere."* Through the years the Lord would speak to Ed through dreams. I'll always believe Ed knew what was ahead of him.

You know, if we're a Christian, God speaks to all of us if we'll take time to listen. So many times we hurry through our prayers and don't give Him time to talk to us.

During this time of your life I encourage you to pray and listen. Listen and He'll guide you down new roads. Listen and He'll whisper sweet words of love and encouragement to your spirit. Just listen.

JOURNAL ENTRY - MARCH 12, 2010

"Dear Father in Heaven, You are my everything. My hope, my trust is in You. I thank You for the miracle You are doing in Ed's life. I thank You that there will be a financial

abundance - every need will be met. I thank You for family and friends who know how to pray. I thank You for knowing my heart and for the relationship we have. I worship You because of who You are. Thank You for all you have done, thank you for all you are doing, thank you for all you will do. There is none like you!"

CHAPTER FIVE

The Nightmare Continues

As we are waiting for the oncologist to find Ed a bed in one of the cancer hospitals, he continued to get worse. His pain medication was so strong it caused severe hallucinations. Rachael and I spent many sleepless nights trying to convince him there were no mice in his bed or spiders in the room. I would have never made it through those times without her by my side. Some nights we would have to walk him from the bed to his recliner where he'd sleep maybe an hour before we'd move him back to the bed.

It was hard to get him to eat but we tried to keep him hydrated. On March 23rd, after a couple of extremely hard days, we took him back to the emergency room. They did another CT scan and found that the tumor was growing and it was pushing on his liver.

The next day the oncologist informed us they'd found a bed for him and they transferred him by ambulance to the new hospital. When we got there his oncologist explained how serious his cancer was – stage 4 – and it would have to be treated aggressively with extremely strong chemotherapy. He told us that there was only a thirty percent chance that he would survive. That was okay. We knew God was going to heal him.

A PIC line was put in his arm to be used when receiving his chemo. They did a bone marrow biopsy.

They determined what drugs to use and he received his first treatment that day. His liver began to respond almost immediately. If he continued to get better, he'd go home in two days. He would need eight treatments.

All went well and he did go home. That night the nausea and vomiting began. I gave him his medicine and he ate crackers and drank some tea. This would be the routine for several days.

It's hard to be a care giver especially to someone you love with all of your heart. You hate they're sick and suffering and you can't do anything about it. You pray for their healing and try to do everything in your power to make them feel better, to make them comfortable. But some days their pain is too great and you fail. And they're in so much pain and feel so hopeless that they take that despair and pain out on you. They say words they don't mean. The pain is talking and you realize that but it still hurts.

That's when you just have to pray and try to put yourself in their shoes for just a little while. Imagine their frustration. Everything they loved to do can't be done anymore. Each breath, each step feels like they are running a marathon.

Imagine how hard it is for them to "stay positive" when their pain level is a nine out of ten. When they can't eat because their throat looks like ground hamburger from the chemo they've had. When *everything* they do requires help.

Do their words hurt? Yes. But just remember it's the pain - not them - talking.

JOURNAL ENTRY - MARCH 31, 2010

"The first clinic appointment is today. Ed had a pretty good night but I think he was worried about the appointment today. When we get there they take his vitals, everything looks good. He can have his next treatment.

It's a strange feeling to walk into a room and see about ten people receiving their treatments at the same time. Today it was mostly women. It only took about 45 minutes for him to receive his treatment."

The next few days were good. He was able to eat more and stay up for longer periods of time. But it didn't last for long.

JOURNAL ENTRY - GOOD
FRIDAY, APRIL 2, 2010

"Never has Good Friday meant more to me than this year. To think that our precious Savior was crucified for my salvation and that He was beaten and whipped for the healing of all our diseases! How could I ever repay

Him? By believing and accepting that salvation and healing for our bodies. Ed is healed. I know beyond a shadow of a doubt he is. Thank you Jesus for your sacrifice of love."

Ed's temperature began to go up every night (which is a symptom of the cancer). He became dehydrated and had to go to the clinic for IV fluids.

JOURNAL ENTRY - APRIL 5, 2010

"It's time for his blood test. When we get there they diagnose that he needs two units of blood. It takes seven hours for the treatment. It's midnight before he's finished. We get home about 2:30 a.m. He has a doctor's appointment scheduled for that day, (Tuesday), but we move it to the next day. They are concerned with his liver."

We hadn't celebrated Easter with the family, so they were coming over that evening for dinner. His sister, Faye, and her daughter, Kait, had flown in from California to check on him. I spent the day cooking and cleaning and looking forward to having everyone together. The sad part was Ed didn't feel like eating anything. He spent most of the evening in bed, but he did get up and sit in his recliner for awhile. He wanted to have prayer with everyone. The sweet Presence of the Lord was with us.

JOURNAL ENTRY - APRIL 7, 2010

"His liver function is so bad they immediately admit him to the hospital. His file is marked 'critical.' His skin tone is yellow. The doctor tells us that the cancer has grown and a more aggressive treatment is needed – and it has horrific side effects. It is very hard on the body, but Ed agrees to have the treatment."

What a shock! I still believed the promise God gave me so even though it looked bad, *It will be well.* Ed began treatment that day. It was a four-day regimen.

When you know unless God heals you you're gonna die, you search your heart to be sure it's clean when you stand before Him. Late one night Ed became very agitated. He felt he needed to ask forgiveness from two people and he wanted me to contact them immediately so he could do that. I sent the emails that night and his conscious was clear. He became peaceful and before he went to sleep he said "God knows my heart".

He had the opportunity to say "I'm sorry" but what if he hadn't had that time? I wonder how many of us have said words we shouldn't have said and done things we shouldn't have done? We need to ask someone to forgive us but keep putting it off. We are not guaranteed tomorrow. Take care of it today. If you meet God today, you want to meet Him with a clean heart.

The days turned into weeks and at this point Ed had been in the hospital for two weeks. We had a scare on April 24th. His blood pressure dropped to 80/40 and the rapid response team was called in. He had severe pain in his chest, so they did an EKG. They also ordered a lung scan and ultrasounds of his heart and legs.

I really believe Ed thought he was dying that night. He made me call Mom and Dad so I wouldn't be there by myself if he died. No matter how bad he was feeling, he would always ask me how I was – everyday – as I sat by his side. He was always concerned about me, even in the midst of his pain. That's true love.

The EKG was fine. The pain was not a heart attack. His lung scan was fine, but the scan of his legs found blood clots in his right leg from his knee to his ankle. They started him on blood thinners. I found out later that it would have taken at least six months for the blood clots to dissolve.

JOURNAL ENTRY - APRIL 20, 2010

"The past few days all run together with medicines and the routine of the hospital. He isn't sleeping and hates taking medicine. Even water hurts his throat and he is losing so much weight they decide to put a feeding tube in.

Almost immediately he began to feel better and stronger. After a couple of days he was able to walk down the hall a short distance. I was so excited! God is hearing our prayers."

CHAPTER SIX

One Day at a Time

If I had known that April 26th would be the last day Ed would ever speak to me how different it would have been. I would have said so many things from my heart. I'd be sure he knew how much I loved him. How awesome a father he was to our children. How proud of him I was. The day started off good. The doctor's visit went well and he had walked to the nurses' station. That was a major accomplishment for him.

About noon he began to feel tired so he got into bed for a nap. As I helped him into bed, he reached for me and hugged me and said, *"I love you so much and I owe you so much"*. My response was *"I love you and you owe me nothing"*. That would be our last conversation.

He napped about two hours and then woke up irritated. Something wasn't right. I called the nurse who came in and she immediately called in the head nurse. They began to ask him simple questions and when he couldn't answer them, they called for the Rapid Response team to evaluate him.

As they were evaluating him, he fell over to one side of the bed and began choking. They called *code blue* and within minutes the room was filled with about 25 doctors and nurses. They made me wait in the hall. I called my mother to tell her what was happening and I couldn't talk for crying. She called my brother, Greg, to come to the hospital to be with me. One of the nurses came to get me and took me back into the room. I am so thankful for nurses who become your family during times like this. They thought maybe part of the blood clot had gone to his lungs. He was moved to the Intensive Care Unit.

The first night in the ICU went on forever. He was having trouble breathing, so he was put on a ventilator. They took out his PIC line. They thought it might be infected. Every time I went to check on him during the night his nurse would tell me how critical his condition was. I know they were trying to prepare me for what might happen. But I still didn't believe it. *It will be well.* That night was spent in prayer and people all over the country prayed with us.

He would spend thirteen days in the ICU. On his second day there, five of his major organs began to shut down. We were living *one day at a time.* He was losing blood. In a 36-hour period he had been given 36 blood products. As fast as they put the blood in, it would come out. They found that his stomach was full of tiny pinholes from the chemotherapy. He received treatment for this and the blood loss slowed down.

His doctors suggested that we start reducing his medicines and the blood intake. They recommended letting nature run its course. To let him die. We asked them to continue to do everything they could for him until his family from Louisiana could come up and see him. They agreed to continue to do all they could for him.

"Ed makes it through another night. We are still surviving one day at a time. It's Thursday now and I met with his oncologist who proceeds to tell me that he wants to start reducing his meds and his blood products. I listen and then tell him what the children and I have decided – continue full force through the weekend. I tell him that Ed's family is coming in and I want them to have some time with him. The doctor agrees and the treatment continues."

When someone you love is fighting for their life, nothing else matters. Everything else in your life ceases to exist, to matter. That's how it was on Sunday, May 2nd, as the great flood hit Nashville and its surrounding areas. I woke up in the ICU waiting room to the sound of the news anchormen warning people about the flood.

A few minutes later an announcement comes over the hospital PA system for everyone on the ground floor of the parking garage to move their cars to a higher level. I heard all of this and saw the news in a fog. I looked out of the hospital window to see the rain continuing to pour but not truly comprehending what was going on.

You see, in my world my sweetheart was fighting

for his life. His family had come from California and Louisiana to see him and I needed to be strong for all of them. To reassure them that *It will be well* even though it didn't look like it at that time.

Throughout the day the weather continued to get worse. The roads around the hospital were flooded. No one was able to get in or out. Ed's doctor walked the last couple of miles to the hospital in the pouring rain and flood waters so he could get to the hospital to check on his patients.

One of the women waiting with me in the ICU for news about her husband was told that her house was flooded. I remember thinking how awful it was that she had lost her home and would possibly lose her husband.

Later that week people would come by to check on Ed and would talk about everything going on with the flood and I would politely listen but I would be thinking *none of this matters, it's just stuff, it can be replaced.*

For those of you who have lost someone you love, you understand how I felt. You lose track of time. You don't always know what day it is. Your world revolves around their blood count, their blood pressure, their heart rate, their pain level. It's all about their needs and you try to think of something, anything you can do to help them. But sometimes all you can do is hold their hand, sing to them and pray.

I knew when I woke up that morning (May 8th) that there was something different about that day. I now know it was God preparing me. I went into Ed's ICU room to find his blood pressure was very low. They were giving him medicine to help raise it. He continued to get worse as the day progressed. By the time evening arrived it was taking everything in him (even with the help of the ventilator) to breathe. Everything was shutting down.

All of the family had been to see us that day. With a heavy heart I ask Alan to call all the family to let them know what was happening – Ed was going home.

One by one the children and I say our final goodbyes. I always believed that even though Ed couldn't respond he could hear and understand us. So we each had our time alone with him to share our hearts. To let him know how much he's loved. After we each had our time, the nurse administered the morphine that would ease the pain.

It's 1:40 a.m. on Sunday, Mother's Day. Along with us, Mom, Dad, Greg and Diane are around his bedside. I stood by his head and talked to him and kissed him on his arm three times for *I love you*, something I began when he was moved to the ICU and the only place that I could kiss that didn't have a tube in the way was his arm.

Many nights when he was in pain and the medicine wasn't working he'd ask me to sing to him. It would help him relax and he'd go to sleep. He would tell the nurses the next day, *my angel sang me to sleep last night*. So on this night with his family around him we began to sing *In the Presence of Jehovah*. I told him we were okay – that we'd be fine. He could go home. At 2:22 a.m. he took his last breath on earth and his first in Heaven.

JOURNAL ENTRY - MAY 9, 2010

"We all say our goodbyes. I kiss his warm body one last time with my code

25

kisses 'I love you'. I tell the nurses and hospital staff thank you for all they've done. With that said we leave the ICU where we have been for thirteen days and the hospital where I have lived since April 7th."

CHAPTER SEVEN

One Hour at a Time

Even in the midst of everything that my eyes were seeing, the blood loss, the organs shutting down, I still believed Ed would be healed! So imagine my pain when on May 9, 2010, at 2:22 a.m. (only two months after his diagnosis) Ed left this earth for his home in Heaven. That's not the way it was supposed to end. God told me that *I would get through it*. At the time He spoke it, I thought He meant Ed and I would get through it. But now, I understand that wasn't God's plan. I'd get through it…*even if*.

When you go from totally believing God is going to heal someone you love to looking at their lifeless body, it is almost too much to physically bear. If you don't have Christ in your life, I feel sorry for you. I know the only reason I'm here today is because of my relationship with Christ and the love and prayers of my family and friends. I pray that if you don't have a relationship with Him you will before the next hour has come and gone. His love will help ease your pain.

From the time Ed was admitted to the hospital on April 7th until he passed on May 9th I was with him. I left the hospital once for two hours when he was in the ICU, but other than that I was with him. My children and I slept every night in the ICU waiting room. Every chance we had we were with him.

One of the hardest things I've ever had to do was to

leave his body at the hospital and go home without him. I knew he was in Heaven. You see, I believe to be absent from the body is to be present with the Lord. So I knew he was in the presence of God and our loved ones who were in Heaven. He was healed and whole, no more pain or suffering.

The question was *What do I do now? How do I get through this? Lord, you told me I'd get through this and I would share my story and it would bring glory to you. But how do I start?*

You begin with prayer. You pray. Pray for the strength to make it through the next hour. And when you make it through that hour, thank God and ask Him to help you through the next hour. And when you do, thank God and ask Him to help you through the next hour. Get the picture?

JOURNAL ENTRY - MAY 9, 2010

"I am in shock. I can't believe this is really happening. But it is. Alan and Amber came home with me and Rachael. We got home around 4 a.m. I climb in bed and try to sleep. I haven't been in a bed in awhile and it's kind of hard to get used to. At 8:30 a.m. the funeral home calls. The nightmare continues."

I remember that first night of being home and back in my bed without Ed like it was yesterday. I remember the tears flowing and talking to God asking Him, pleading with Him to give me the strength to make it through the next day. Through all the funeral arrangements, through all of the necessary phone calls, through everything that *first day* would bring.

This was the prayer I prayed for many, many nights. And God was always faithful. He always helped me get through that day. And He'll do the same for you.

When you don't know how you'll make it, when it's hard to take the next breath, pray this prayer: "Father, I love you with all my heart and I know you love me. I need you to help me make it through this day. Whatever it holds, help me. I know I can trust in you...*even if.*"

JOURNAL ENTRY - MAY 12, 2010

"It's Wednesday, May 12th, and it's time for the family visitation. God spoke to my heart and told me to pray with our kids before we went in to see Ed, so I did. Through my tears I thanked God for Ed and prayed for the strength we would need to make it through the days ahead."

CHAPTER EIGHT
Overcoming Guilt

JOURNAL ENTRY - MAY 20, 2010

"I have visited the gravesite every day since we laid your body there, baby. I know you're not there, but it makes it a little easier to go there and talk to you. Of course, I talk to you around the house too. I've told myself I will give myself a month to do this."

For five and a half months I visited Ed's grave every day. Sometimes it would be midnight, but I'd get in my car and drive the seven or eight miles just to be where his body was.

For almost three years I couldn't take a deep breath without my heart reacting like I'd been crying too long and couldn't get my breath. It was a physical, as well as emotional pain. My heart was broken. It's true that you never know how much you love someone until they're gone. You know you love them, but you don't really understand how deep that love is until you don't have them.

I know if you are like me, you've spent hours blaming yourself. Asking yourself questions like, *Why didn't I make him go to the doctor sooner?* Or *Why didn't I realize he was sick sooner?* Why didn't I? If only I had . . .

As I told you earlier, I didn't leave the hospital. I felt like something might happen and I would be needed to make a decision or to sign a treatment form (which had happened many times). When you're in that situation you pray you make the right decision, that you make the right choice.

On the evening before Ed passed, my brother, Greg, and his wife, Diane, were visiting us at the hospital. He took me to the side and reminded me that God was sovereign. Now I had heard that word before. You see, I was raised in church. I am blessed to have been raised in a Christian home with loving parents. And I knew that God was sovereign. But what exactly does the word *sovereign* mean?

I didn't really research its meaning until several weeks later, but when I did it helped with the guilt from the *what if's*. The definition of sovereign is *a supreme ruler possessing supreme or ultimate power.* Simply saying, *God is in control.* There is absolutely nothing that is outside of His influence and authority.

No matter what decision I made concerning Ed's treatment or care, God was in control. God ultimately wanted the best for Ed. My decisions, right or wrong, didn't change that. Once I understood that, the *what ifs* didn't hurt me as bad and now, five years after his passing, I accept that God's plan is always the right plan. He is in control. His ways are always best.

Forgive yourself and trust the one and only sovereign God. . .*even if.*

CHAPTER NINE

Life Goes On

Ed always felt like once you had done what God put you on earth to do, He would take you home with Him. He debated this with many people through the years (and they didn't always agree with him) but he always believed it.

A very dear friend and pastor's wife told me this story when I asked her to pray for Ed's healing. She told me that one time she was praying for a man in their church who had been diagnosed with cancer. He was a middle-aged man, a good man who was a minister and had a loving family who didn't want to lose him. So as she was praying for his healing she heard the voice of God speak to her as clearly as she had ever heard Him speak before. He said to her, *"Why would you want me to heal him when he's done what I put him on earth to do and he could be in Heaven with me?"*

Wow! That went along with how Ed felt about life. And it's so true. We want them here with us. We can't even imagine life without them. We ask them to go through painful treatments and procedures so we can have them here with us. But maybe they've done what they were put on earth to do. Why would we want to keep them from Heaven? How amazing and beautiful Heaven must be! To meet Jesus face to face and to see all of our loved ones again. No pain, no sickness, no sorrow – only peace and love.

The evening of Ed's passing, when we knew his fight

was almost over, one of his nurses began to talk to me. She knew I was having trouble accepting what was ahead of me. Remember, I believed God was going to heal Ed and we would travel the country telling of his miraculous healing and the healing power of God. She asked me if I believed in Heaven. I told her yes and that Ed was a minister. She just smiled and began to tell me her story.

When she was 24 she went to the dentist to have her wisdom teeth out. Something went wrong and she died. She went to heaven where she saw such beautiful colors and light and saw people around her who were coming to welcome their loved ones. Everybody was happy. She talked about all the beautiful colors and the joy she felt. She was watching everything that was going on around her when a little girl came to her and told her that she had to go back, it wasn't her time yet. But she didn't want to come back. But the little girl told her that she had to, that she would need her some day. And so she came back to earth.

She was 54 at the time she told me this and she never had children, but this child she saw in heaven was her brother's child that she was helping to raise. She told me, "He will be in a much better place, do not worry. He will leave here and be in Heaven."

Another sweet nurse hugged me as I broke down in tears in the hallway outside his room and asked me if I would like her to pray with me. I said yes and she began to pray for my peace and strength.

I am so thankful that in the midst of my pain, in my darkest hour, God was with me holding me in His arms through the arms of the ICU nurses.

JOURNAL ENTRY

"I keep remembering what Ed made me promise him on one of those nights when he was hurting so badly. He wanted me to help him write his will, but I joked it off and told him he wasn't going to need it any time soon. He told me to 'listen to him'. He said, 'Don't let them keep bringing me back.' I asked him to repeat it and he did. Then he said, 'You know what I mean' and I said 'Yes baby, I know and I won't' never thinking I would have to make that choice. But really Ed was making that choice for me. His body was making that choice for me."

So where do I go from here? The life I had planned had changed. The dreams we had to travel on our 35th wedding anniversary wouldn't happen. The plans to sell our home and build another one with our own hands would never happen. There were so many unfulfilled dreams and plans.

After Ed's home going service, Rachael and I decided to visit the churches of the four pastors who spoke at his service. We wanted to show our love and appreciation to them in this way. One of those pastor's wives had sent me a beautiful card that basically said, *"You know Ed wouldn't want you to stop working for the Lord. He would want you to continue in the ministry."*

Ed and I never talked about him dying. We always spoke of his healing and positive things so we never had the *This is what I want you to do when I'm gone* conversation. I sometimes wish we had, but I know at that time I wouldn't have allowed him to even mention the possibility that he was going to die. But when you've been married to someone for 33 years and you go-together for three years before you were married, you know how they think. Sometimes you think you share the same brain! And I knew what she said was true.

I didn't *get busy* immediately. The first few weeks you walk around in a daze just trying to get through each day. Then you start going through all of the *firsts*. The first holiday, the first wedding anniversary without them, their birthday, your birthday, etc. You're relieved when you get through them. When that first year and the anniversary of their death has passed you think, "*Thank God I've made it through the first year*" only to realize that the second year is as hard or harder than the first year because you've realized that it's not a nightmare you've been having, but your life. They're not coming back.

Somewhere between the first and second year God opened a door for me to serve as the minister of music at Amazing Grace Ministries, the very church whose pastor's wife gave me the encouraging word to continue to work for the Lord. After praying about it for several weeks, I committed to serving there. My oldest daughter, Rachael, agreed to go with me each weekend as the church was two and a half hours from our home.

It was hard in the beginning, but we had several friends there who just loved us as we tried to find our place to work for God. We were trying to figure out what the new *normal* was for our lives. Once you lose someone you love, life is never normal again. Things you did as a couple or a family are never the same again. You just have to continue to have family time and make new memories and eventually *normal* comes back, even if it is a different *normal*.

Being involved in God's work has saved my life in so many ways. It has helped fill many hours as I worked on music or prepared lessons for our children's ministry. Four years ago Rachael and I began our summer youth camps again. I know Ed would be proud of all of us.

If it helped me, it will help you too. Get involved in your church or local charity. There are always places you can serve. Help someone - it'll help you in return. Share your story with someone it may help them to go on… *even if*.

CHAPTER TEN

God is Faithful

So where do I go from here? I still believe that God is the great physician. That He heals all diseases. I still believe there is *nothing* too hard for my God. I still believe He hears and answers my prayers. I still believe He loves me more than I can even imagine and that someday I'll meet Him face to face. I believe He wants what's best for me, even when I don't understand what that is.

I wrote a worship chorus a few months ago that simply says:

Lord, I believe, I believe you're blessing me
Lord, I believe, I believe you're blessing me
I believe
Even when the storm clouds roll
Lord, your touch restores my soul
I believe, I believe

And I do believe. Even in the midst of the pain of losing my husband, God has blessed me. I've come to know Him in ways I didn't before. I trust Him to guide me in decisions I now have to make on my own. I've bought my first house on my own. I've bought my first car on my own. He's with me every hour of every day. I am never alone. I feel Him with me always.

He has blessed my business for many years. He recently

blessed me with a full-time ministry job. He has blessed my children and now I have grandchildren (two beautiful granddaughters, Charlotte Rose and Lylah Harper, and a handsome grandson, Seth Alan). When I look in their sweet faces I see Ed and I thank God for them even more.

This fall will bring the arrival of another wonderful granddaughter, Arabella Grace! We don't know yet when her arrival will be, but I can assure you – she will be greatly loved!

Am I *over* the loss of my husband? No! Probably never will be, but I can take a deep breath without my heart skipping a beat now. I can look at old pictures and *remember* without always crying. I can talk about him with a smile on my face without there always being tears.

I am blessed to have had a husband who taught me how to take care of myself. I can check the air in my tires and check my oil. I can take care of minor plumbing problems. I can even install a commode! So many things he taught me to do that I never in a million years thought I would ever need to know. But God knew. He knew Ed's time would be short and that I would need to know how to be self-sufficient. God knew.

JOURNAL ENTRY - MAY 17, 2010

"Ed, you have been such an awesome husband, father and man of God. You have taught me how to do so much. How to be self-sufficient. I never wanted to do this on my own, but I can, thanks to

you. You've touched not only our lives, but you've touched hundreds of others throughout the years. We will never forget you."

I am thankful for my relationship with my children. There are not enough words to express to them how much I love them and how much I appreciate them walking through this with me. They have all been walking through their own seasons of grief, learning how to live without a father who loved them so much and who taught them how to be amazing, self-sufficient women and men.

I'll never forget the words my sweet daughter, Amber, spoke to me on the evening that we knew we were going to lose Ed. She said, *"When you think about eternity, this time away from him will be nothing. When you think of all the time we'll have when we get to heaven, this time apart is nothing."* And that is so true. No matter how long your loved one has been gone, it will seem like just a moment when you meet again in heaven!

Grief steals your joy. It robs you of your hope. It brings to a halt your plans for the future. It changes everything.

"They" tell you there are five stages of grief: denial, anger, bargaining with God, depression and acceptance. God says "to everything there is a season" (Ephesians 3:1 King James Version). "They" tell you it usually takes about eight years to go through these stages. God says "your latter will be more blessed than your beginning" (Job 42:12 King James Version).

It's been over five years since Ed went home. That's

more than enough time to grieve. He would tell me to "get on with life". He would tell me "to quit wasting time". So I'm going to listen to his voice speaking to my heart. I refuse to grieve any more. I will always love him. I will always miss him and his sweet smile, but it is time to get my life back. It is time to get my joy back. It's time to see what God has in store for me, for the rest of *my* life. I am not guaranteed tomorrow. How can I make my life count today?

As you go through your stages of grief I encourage you - don't give up! Keep trusting in God. He will help you through each and every hard day, through every new situation you have to go through. Through every new thing you have to learn to do on your own. You will get through this! One hour at a time, one day at a time... *even if* the healing didn't come on this earth and your life will never be *normal* again and there are unfulfilled dreams...He is still the sovereign God and He loves you more than you can ever imagine! Stay strong in Him... *even if.*

JOURNAL ENTRY - MAY 17, 2010

"Baby, you've completed the journey. God healed you in Heaven. No more pain, no more heartaches. Nothing but love and light and laughter. Someday I'll see you there! Save some hugs for me. I LOVE YOU!"

With heartfelt thanks to my girls. . .

. . . Rachael, thank you for all of the time spent typing and tweaking *Even If.* Thank you for encouraging me to share even more of our story than I had planned. Thank you for listening to the voice of God when He gave you the plan for financing and publishing *Even If.* Your love, support and encouragement mean more than you'll ever know. I love you more and I am blessed to have you as my daughter!

. . . Amber, thank you for proof-reading *Even If* and reminding me that "God doesn't call the equipped, He equips the called". Those encouraging words have helped me so many times when I began to question this assignment from God. Your love, support and encouragement mean more than you'll ever know. I love you more and I am blessed to have you as my daughter!

And to my guys. . .

. . . Alan, thank you for encouraging me to continue with the business Dad started. You've been my sounding board when I needed advice on the business and my personal affairs as well. Thank you for answering all of my many questions. Your love, support and encouragement mean more than you'll ever know. I love you more and I am blessed to have you as my son!

. . . Ryan, thank you for encouraging me to follow my dream as you follow yours. For being my extra pair of hands to help with whatever job I needed help with at the time. Thanks for climbing the ladders that were too tall for me. Your love, support and encouragement mean more than you'll ever know. I love you more and I am blessed to have you as my son!

For additional copies or if you would like prayer for you or someone you love, please contact me at Deborahripley58@yahoo.com.

May God's love and blessings surround you today . . . EVEN IF.

Family Photos

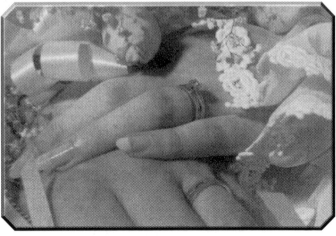

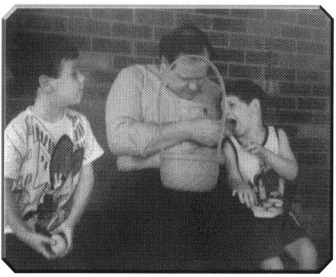

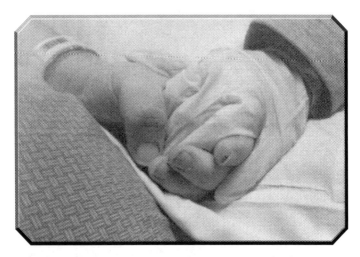

Dec 26, 201
12:56PM

64

Printed in the United States
By Bookmasters